ARCTIC OCEAN
SEVERNAYA ZEMLYA
FRANZ JOSEF
NEW SIBERIAN ISLANDS
Wrangel Island
NOVAYA
FINLAND
RUSSIA
ESTONIA
LATVIA
LITHUANIA
BELARUS
UKRAINE
MOLDOVA
ROMANIA
BULGARIA
KAZAKHSTAN
MONGOLIA
GEORGIA
UZBEKISTAN
KRYGYSTAN
NORTH KOREA
GREECE
TURKEY
ARMENIA
AZERBAIJAN
TURKMENISTAN
TAJIKISTAN
JAPAN
NORTH PACIFIC OCEAN
CHINA
SOUTH KOREA
CYPRUS
SYRIA
IRAQ
IRAN
AFGHANISTAN
JORDAN
KUWAIT
PAKISTAN
NEPAL
EGYPT
QATAR
UNITED ARAB EMIRATES
BANGLADESH
SAUDI ARABIA
OMAN
INDIA
MYANMAR (BURMA)
LAOS
ERITREA
YEMEN
THAILAND
VIETNAM
CAMBODIA
PHILIPPINES
GUAM
SUDAN
DJIBOUTI
ETHIOPIA
ADAMAN ISLANDS (INDIA)
NICOBAR ISLANDS (INDIA)
FEDERATED STATES OF MICRONESIA
MARSHALL ISLANDS
CENTRAL AFRICAN REPUBLIC
SOMALIA
MALDIVES
SRI LANKA
MALAYSIA
BRUNEI
DEM. REP. OF THE CONGO
UGANDA
KENYA
RWANDA
BURUNDI
KIRIBATI
TANZANIA
SEYCHELLES
INDONESIA
PAPUA NEW GUINEA
SOLOMON ISLANDS
TUVALU
COMOROS
ZAMBIA
MALAWI
SAMOA
VANUATU
FIJI
MOZAMBIQUE
MAURITIUS
TONGA
ZIMBABWE
BOTSWANA
MADAGASCAR
REUNION
INDIAN OCEAN
AUSTRALIA
NEW CALEDONIA (FRANCE)
SWAZILAND
SOUTH AFRICA
LESOTHO
NEW ZEALAND
PRINCE EDWARD ISLANDS
ILES CROZET (FRANCE)
KERGUELEN ISLAND (FRANCE)

GLOBETROTTERS
AUSTRALIA
Keith Dawson
REDBACK
publishing

First Published 2024 by
Redback Publishing
PO Box 357 Frenchs Forest NSW 2086
Australia

www.redbackpublishing.com
orders@redbackpublishing.com

ISBN 978-1-761400-50-6

Author: Keith Dawson
Editor: Words at Work
Design: Redback Publishing

Original illustrations © Redback Publishing 2024
Originated by Redback Publishing

A catalogue record for this book is available from the National Library of Australia

Acknowledgements
Abbreviations: l–left, r–right, b–bottom, t–top, c–centre, m–middle
We would like to thank the following for permission to reproduce photographs:
(Images © shutterstock, wikimediacommons) Front cover, boomerang, Rama, CC BY-SA 4.0 <https://creativecommons.org/licenses/by-sa/4.0>, via Wikimedia Commons, 4tr bmphotographer/Shutterstock.com, p5bl NigelSpiers/Shutterstock.com, p6bl ArliftAtoz2205/Shutterstock.com, p8ml FiledIMAGE/Shutterstock.com, p9mr ChameleonsEye/Shutterstock.com, p9bl ChameleonsEye/Shutterstock.com, p10tr Philip Schuber/Shutterstock.com, p10bl Joseph Lycett, Public domain, via Wikimedia Commons, p11tc https://www.flickr.com/photos/82134796@N03/denisbin (CC BY-ND 2.0), p12tl E. Phillips Fox, Public domain, via Wikimedia Commons, p12tr Samuel Thomas Gill, Public domain, via Wikimedia Commons, p12br Mitch Ames, CC BY-SA 4.0 <https://creativecommons.org/licenses/by-sa/4.0>, via Wikimedia Commons, p13tl#1 Gary Houston, CC0, via Wikimedia Commons, p13tl#2 Dietmar Rabich/Wikimedia Commons/"Darwin (AU), Bombing of Darwin 1942 Memorial -- 2019 -- 4358"/CC BY-SA 4.0, p13tr#1 neftali/Shutterstock.com, p13tr#2 HREOC, CC BY 2.0 <https://creativecommons.org/licenses/by/2.0>, via Wikimedia Commons, p14tl Fabi Mingrino/Shutterstock.com, p14br Premier's Department, State Public Relations Bureau, Photographic Unit, Public domain, via Wikimedia Commons, p15br Vegemite jar, Lipowski Milan/Shutterstock.com, p16tr ChameleonsEye/Shutterstock.com, p16ml Featureflash Photo Agency/Shutterstock.com, p16bc Unknown author, Public domain, via Wikimedia Commons, p17bl Australian Human Rights Commission, CC BY 2.0 <https://creativecommons.org/licenses/by/2.0>, via Wikimedia Commons, p18br Flickerd, CC BY-SA 4.0 <https://creativecommons.org/licenses/by-sa/4.0>, via Wikimedia Commons, p19tr The National Guard, CC BY 2.0 <https://creativecommons.org/licenses/by/2.0>, via Wikimedia Commons, p19br IOIO IMAGES/Shutterstock.com, p21tl Thomas Wyness/Shutterstock.com, p26ml Maurizio De Mattei/Shutterstock.com, p26br ChameleonsEye/Shutterstock.com, p29mr GagliardiPhotography/Shutterstock.com, p30tr EQRoy/Shutterstock.com, p31 Aboriginal flag, Save nature and wildlife/Shutterstock.com

CONTENTS

MAP OF AUSTRALIA

Did you know?
There are over 10,000 beaches in Australia.

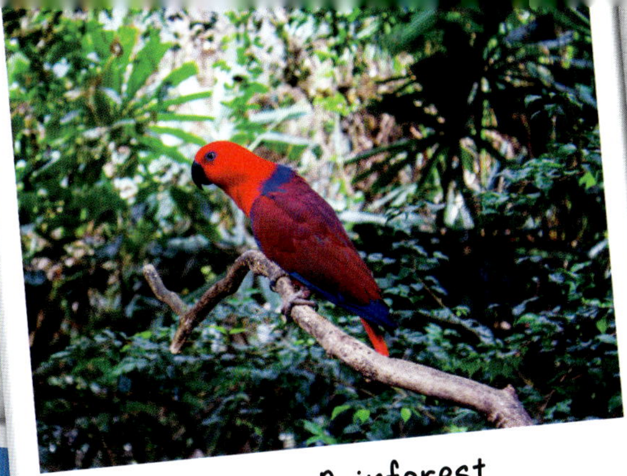

Daintree Rainforest
QUEENSLAND

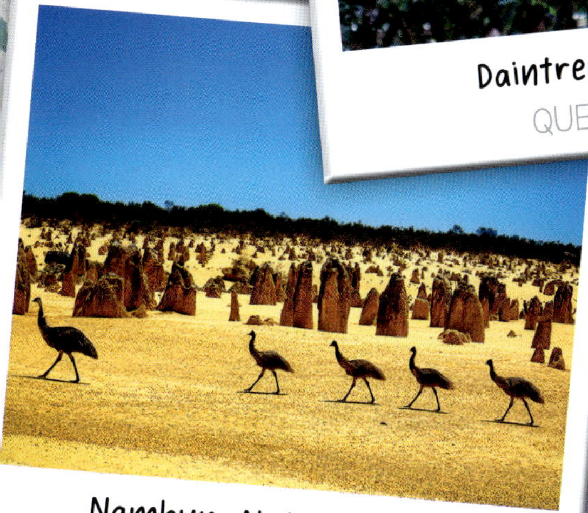

Nambung National Park
WESTERN AUSTRALIA

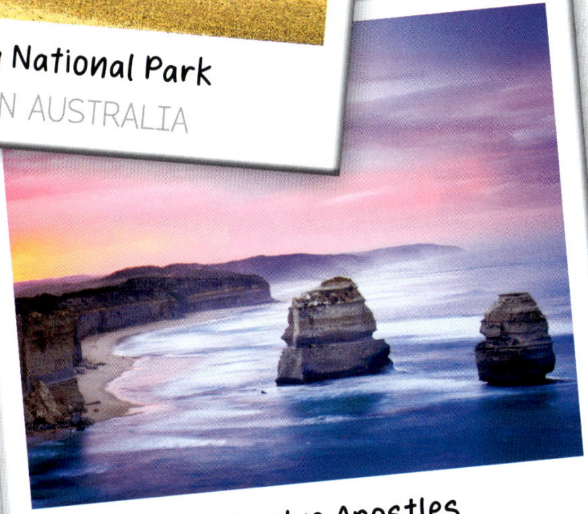

The Twelve Apostles
VICTORIA

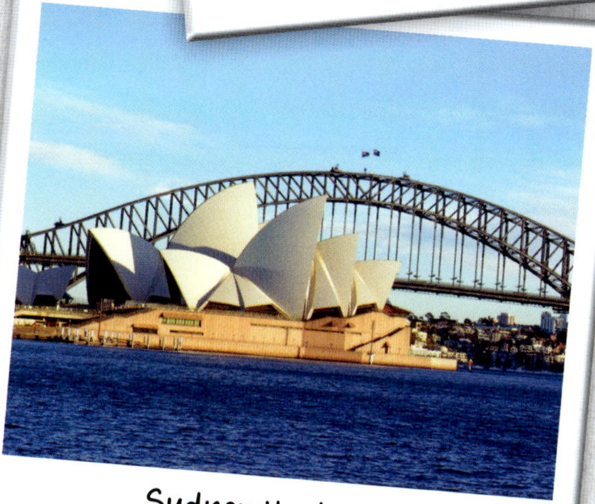

Sydney Harbour
NEW SOUTH WALES

SNAPSHOT

COUNTRY
Australia
(Commonwealth of Australia)

CAPITAL
Canberra

AREA
7,692,024
square kilometres

POPULATION
26,473,055
(ABS 2023)

HIGHEST POINT
Mount Kosciuszko
2,228 metres

NATIONAL LANGUAGE
Australian English
(no official language)

CURRENCY
$ Australian dollar (AUD)

GOVERNMENT
Federal parliamentary constitutional monarchy

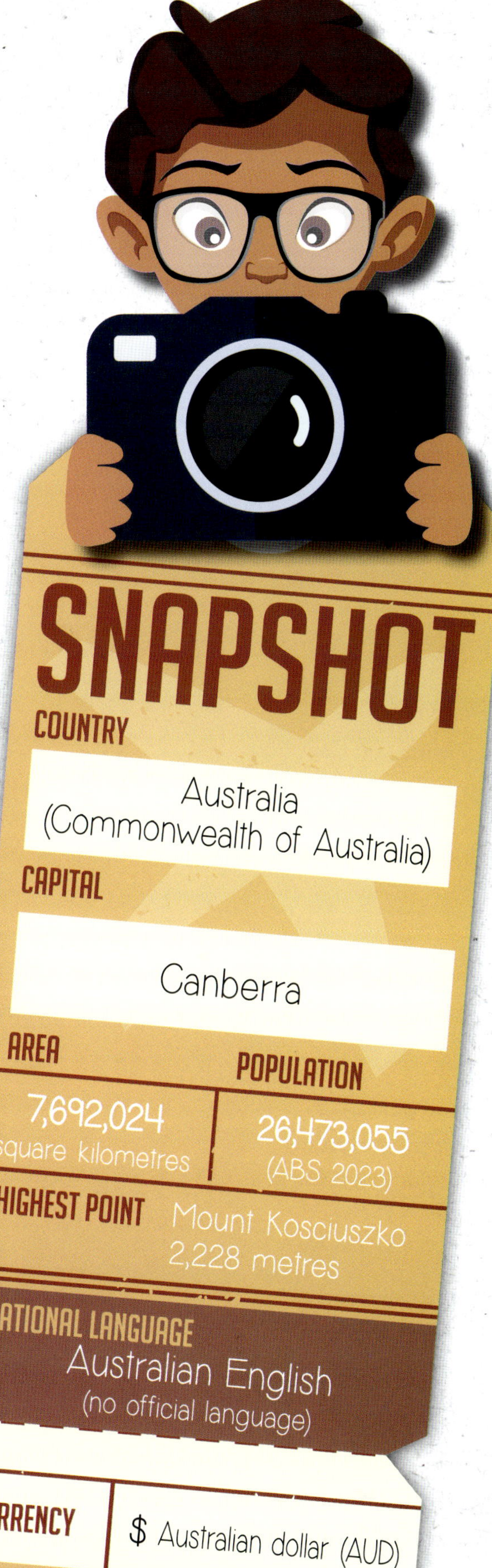

WELCOME TO AUSTRALIA

Australia is both a country and part of the Australian continent. It is the sixth largest country by area in the world, after Russia, Canada, China, the United States and Brazil. It is also one of the driest countries on Earth.

Australia is famed for its diverse natural beauty, particularly its beaches. It has a population of around 26 million people, and most of them live near the coast.

Modern Australia is a multicultural society, with people from many different backgrounds. English is the national language, but there are hundreds of other languages also spoken, including many belonging to Aboriginal and Torres Strait Islander people.

"The Lights of Christmas" projected on St Mary's Cathedral in Sydney

Religion

Australia has no official religion. Christians comprise the largest religious group in Australia, but there are also large Muslim, Hindu, Sikh, Jewish and Buddhist communities.

Australia's States and Territories

Australia is divided into six states and two territories, and each one is unique. Australia has a varied geography, ranging from soaring mountains, to deserts, rainforests and the magnificent Great Barrier Reef.

Canberra is Australia's capital city. It is located within the Australian Capital Territory, which is an area surrounded by the state of New South Wales.

Parliament House
CANBERRA, ACT

How many of Australia's states and territories have you visited?

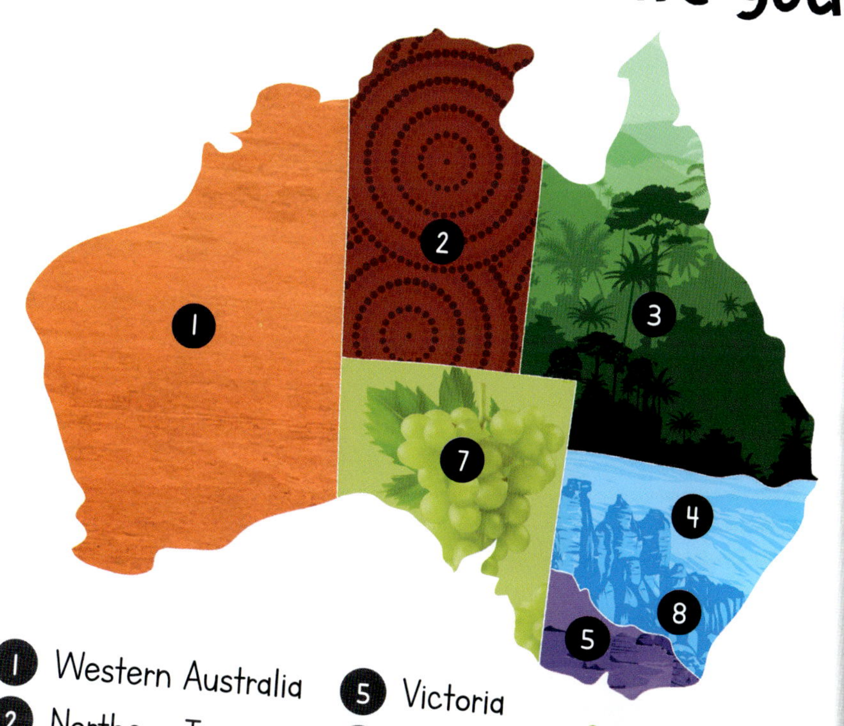

1. Western Australia
2. Northern Territory
3. Queensland
4. New South Wales
5. Victoria
6. Tasmania
7. South Australia
8. Australian Capital Territory

Largest State:
Western Australia (over 2,500,000 square kilometres)

Smallest State:
Tasmania (over 68,000 square kilometres)

Largest Population:
New South Wales (over 8,200,000 people)

GOVERNMENT

Three Levels of Government

Australia has a form of government described as a 'representative democracy'. This means citizens vote for candidates to represent them, make laws and manage government services. Voting is compulsory.

Australia has three levels of government – Federal, State and Local. Each level of government is responsible for different services.

House of Representatives, Parliament House, Canberra

Federal Government

In Australia, federal elections are held approximately every three years. Citizens elect Members of Parliament to represent them in the House of Representatives, and they elect Senators to sit in the Senate. These people represent those who elected them, and they make laws on their behalf.

The Federal Government is responsible for defence, pensions, Medicare, universities, foreign affairs and trade, immigration, national finances, interstate roads and communication, income taxation and its distribution to the States, as well as many other matters concerning Australia and its people.

Did You know?

Australia is also a constitutional monarchy, in which King Charles III is represented locally by the Governor-General.

State and Territory Governments

State and Territory Governments are responsible for schools, hospitals, main roads and police services.

Local Governments

Local governments look after suburban roads, parks, libraries, swimming pools, local planning and building regulations and rubbish removal.

Australia Day

All States and Territories mark Australia Day on 26 January each year. It is a public holiday that allows people to reflect on what it means to be Australian. The date marks the 1788 arrival of the First Fleet which began the European colonisation of Australia. Formal events include citizenship ceremonies, the announcement of Australia Day Honours, flag-raising ceremonies and many other events. Australia Day is viewed by many as a time to reflect on the past and what this day means for Aboriginal and Torres Strait Islander people, who see January 26 as a day of mourning.

ABORIGINAL AND TORRES STRAIT ISLANDER PEOPLE

Australia's Aboriginal and Torres Strait Islander people were the first inhabitants, arriving at least 65,000 years ago. They moved across the country, from the Torres Strait to the far southern tip of Tasmania, taking with them a culture rich with songs, art, dance and deep spiritual beliefs.

Caring for the Land

First Nations people have always cared for the land. They developed a range of land management practices such as leaving areas to recover, rather than depleting all the resources before moving on. They also work with the land, using fire to control the plant growth in areas as a way of reducing the risk of catastrophic bushfires.

Corroborees

Corroborees are spiritual and community events providing opportunities for Aboriginal and Torres Strait Islander people to share ideas and meet people. These events can be public or private and include the ceremonial telling of stories through song and dance.

Did You Know?

There are more than 250 different Aboriginal and Torres Strait Islander languages and many hundreds of dialects spoken across Australia.

Ancient Aquaculture

For thousands of years, the Gunditjmara people of southeastern Australia maintained an extensive aquaculture system along the Tyrendarra lava flow and wetlands at Mt Eccles, now known as the Budj Bim Cultural Landscape.

Budj Bim Cultural Landscape was added to UNESCO's List in August 2019 for its Outstanding Universal Value.

Trapped eels were harvested into baskets

Rock art

A number of the oldest rock art sites in the whole world are in Australia. Some of these sites have been dated to around 50,000 years ago.

Aboriginal Structures

While many Aboriginal and Torres Strait Islander people moved around the land to prevent overuse and protect the delicate balance of nature, there are also examples of permanent structures that were built throughout the country. Many are still visible today, and some are very ancient.

The Brewarrina Fish Traps in New South Wales are one of the oldest man-made structures in the world.

HISTORY BITES

1606, first European landing

In 1606, Dutch explorer Captain Willem Janszoon became the first European to set foot on Australian soil. Over 100 years later, in 1770, Captain James Cook landed at Botany Bay and claimed the land for Great Britain. He also charted the east coast in his ship HMB Endeavour, naming eastern Australia 'New South Wales'. In 1803, English navigator, Matthew Flinders, made the first recorded circumnavigation of Australia.

1850s, Gold Rushes

The discovery of gold in the 1850s had an enormous effect on the development of Australia. So many people from overseas travelled to Australia to seek their fortune on the gold fields, that the population of Australia increased from just 430,000 in 1851 to over 1.7 million twenty years later.

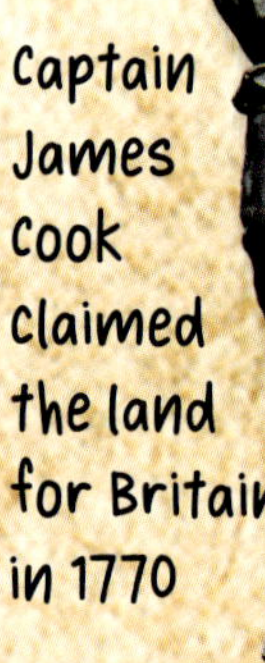

Captain James Cook claimed the land for Britain in 1770

1788, The First Fleet

The First Fleet arrived in 1788 and Captain Arthur Phillip founded a convict settlement in Port Jackson, which is now part of Sydney. The First Fleet consisted of 11 ships carrying about 1,200 marines, officials and other passengers, along with the convicts and crew. Life for them all in the colony was extremely difficult for many years.

1901, Federation of Australia

On 1 January 1901, the British colonies of Queensland, New South Wales, Victoria, Tasmania, South Australia and Western Australia were united when the Constitution of Australia, the set of rules by which Australia is run, came into effect. Together, the former colonies became the states of the Commonwealth of Australia.

A decorative flag celebrating the Federation of Australia

Darwin bombing memorial

Former Prime Minister Kevin Rudd (centre)

1914, The First Anzacs

The First World War began in 1914. At dawn on 25 April 1915, 16,000 Australian and New Zealand soldiers landed on the Gallipoli Peninsula at what is now called Anzac Cove. Thousands of Anzac soldiers were killed or wounded that day. Australians mark the event annually on 25 April with a public holiday called Anzac Day, when they remember the fallen, join marches, and hold commemorative ceremonies.

1942, The Bombing of Darwin

In 1942, during the Second World War, Darwin was bombed by Japanese fighter planes, resulting in destruction across the city and many deaths. This was the largest enemy attack on Australia during the war. The attacks on 19 February were only the first of many more raids made on Darwin between February 1942 and November 1943.

1936, Eddie Koiki Mabo born

Born on Mer (also known as Murray Island) in the Torres Strait in 1936, Eddie Mabo took his claims for traditional land ownership rights to the High Court of Australia. The case lasted ten years, and Eddie Mabo died only six months before the final decision on 3 June 1992, in which the court upheld his claim. This success encouraged other land rights claims by Aboriginal and Torres Strait Islander people across the Nation. Mabo Day is celebrated every year on 3 June.

The Stolen Generations and The Apology

From the early days of settlement until the 1970s, Australian governments forcibly removed many Aboriginal and Torres Strait Islander children from their families and communities. On 13 February 2008, Prime Minister Kevin Rudd made a formal and historic apology in Parliament to Australia's Aboriginal and Torres Strait Islander people. The Apology acknowledged the suffering experienced by the Stolen Generations, caused by laws and official actions that discriminated against them.

SCHOOLS

In Australia, education is free and compulsory for students between the ages of six and sixteen (although there are some differences from State to State).

Surf School

In some coastal areas, children learn to surf as part of their school day.

The education system is divided into primary, secondary and tertiary education. The school year begins in late January and ends in mid-December. There are four terms each year.

The Australian Curriculum includes eight key learning areas: English, Mathematics, Science, Humanities and Social Sciences, Health and Physical Education, Languages, Technologies and the Arts.

School of the Air

In 1951, the first School of the Air was established in Alice Springs. It broadcast lessons by radio to children in isolated Outback areas. Today, remote students in the Australian Outback still receive their schooling from the Alice Springs School of the Air using satellite communication. This unusual school is described as 'the world's largest classroom', with students spread across millions of square kilometres.

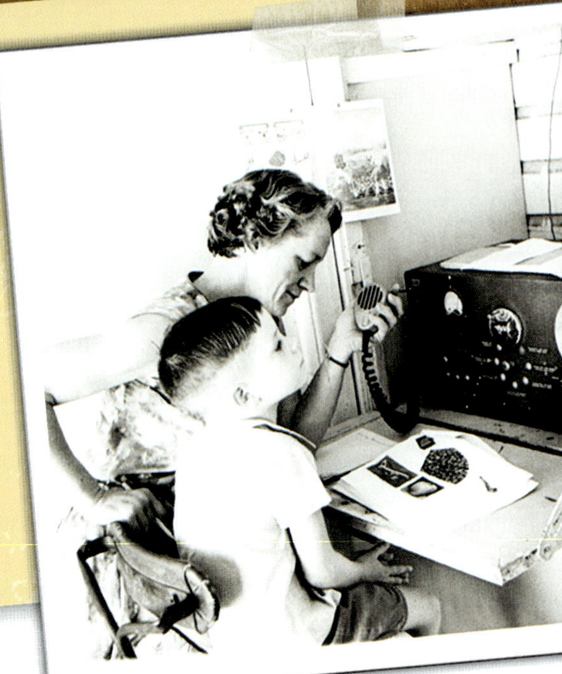

FOOD

Australians enjoy a plentiful supply of fresh foods grown by farmers around the country. As Australia is surrounded by oceans, seafood plays an important role in the local diet. Every day, millions of Australians eat foods produced by the dairy industry, including milk, cream, yogurt and cheese. The farming of beef cattle is a large sector of the food production industry, with beef ending up in local meals, as well as being exported.

Multicultural Cuisine

Australia is a multicultural country, which is reflected in the diverse choice of cuisine available. Not only do Australians eat at European, Asian, Indian and Middle Eastern restaurants, but they also love to cook these cuisines at home.

National Dish

While Australia doesn't have an official national dish, Vegemite is a favourite Aussie food. This brown, salty paste gets spread on toast across millions of homes every day, and over 22 million jars are sold each year.

THE ARTS

Australia has produced many great performers, writers, painters and musicians.

Paul Hogan starred as Crocodile Dundee

Australian Indigenous Art

Aboriginal and Torres Strait Islander artists have been working in Australia for many thousands of years. Many painting styles developed over this long period of time, but the dot painting style is the most recognisable in the international art scene today. These artworks represent Dreaming, maps, food and water sources and people's spiritual connections to the land and its wildlife. Works by leading Aboriginal and Torres Strait Islander artists now hang in national collections and sell for high prices.

The Film Industry

Some Australian movies have had box office success both in Australia as well as overseas. *Crocodile Dundee* (released in 1986) broke box office records in Australia and in the USA. It is still the highest grossing Australian film of all time. One of the earliest feature films ever made, *The Story of the Kelly Gang*, was created in Australia in 1906. In recent years, overseas production companies have been making films in Australia, using local film crews, locations and modern studio facilities.

Australian Children's Literature

Australia has a strong tradition of producing quality children's literature. Ethel Turner (1872-1958) wrote books including *Seven Little Australians* and *The Family at Misrule*, which were amongst the first children's novels set in Australia.

Well-known contemporary authors include Mem Fox, whose picture book *Possum Magic* has been popular since it was published in 1983, selling millions of copies.

Jackie French is a successful writer of picture books, non-fiction and novels for children. Her bestselling picture book, *Diary of a Wombat*, draws on her own experiences looking after wombats.

Vietnamese-born Australian, Anh Do, is not only a bestselling author for children and adults, but also an artist who has been a finalist in the prestigious Archibald Prize.

Bangarra Dance Theatre

The Bangarra Dance Theatre is an Aboriginal and Torres Strait Islander modern dance company, which takes traditional themes and dance styles and combines them with contemporary dance. This produces a unique and exciting theatre experience. Bangarra performs across Australia and around the world.

Australians love their sport and participate in a wide range that includes netball, cricket, soccer, rugby league, rugby union, Aussie Rules and golf.

A SPORTING NATION

Cricket

Cricket is one of Australia's best-loved outdoor games. When the English colonised Australia in 1788, they brought the game of cricket with them. The first organised match is believed to have been played in 1803 by the officers and marines of HMS Calcutta during a visit to Sydney.

Today, thousands of Australian men, women and children play cricket in organised clubs and competitions throughout Australia every year.

Aussie Rules Football

Aussie Rules is a uniquely Australian sport. Developed in Australia, it was influenced by both rugby from Britain, and by marngrook, a local Indigenous ballgame. It is one of the most popular sports in Australia.

Rugby League and Union

There are two codes of rugby: rugby league and rugby union. There are many differences between the two games. They include differences in the points awarded for tries and goals, the number of players on the teams, and the ways scrums are formed and used in the games. Internationally, Australia has long been one of the giants of both the union and league games.

Football (Soccer)

Football (soccer) is a popular club sport in Australia, with many thousands of players across the country. Recent successes by the Australian women's soccer team, the Matildas, have raised the profile of the sport, and encouraged more young players to enjoy the 'beautiful game'.

Swimming

Many of the world's greatest swimmers are Australian. Their medal tallies at each Olympic Games are exceptional for a country with such a comparatively small population.

MAJOR INDUSTRIES

Australia is rich in natural resources and land, so both mining and farming have contributed to the country's economic growth.

Open cut gold mining

Gold Mining

Gold is one of Australia's most important products. In the 1800s, the discovery of gold attracted thousands of new settlers to Australia and led to the establishment and growth of many inland towns and cities. Today, gold exports earn billions of dollars for Australia each year.

Coal Mining

Coal mining is currently one of Australia's most important industries, because it is used to generate electricity. This reliable power source is necessary for the Australian steel industry and for other manufacturing as well. The coal industry employs many thousands of people in mines and in the industries that supply mines, such as machinery, manufacture, transport and maintenance. Coal is one of Australia's main exports, but its effect on climate change has caused many people to criticise its continued use, and to call for more sustainable energy practices.

Wheat Industry

The wheat industry includes wheat farmers and companies that rely on wheat for their livelihood, such as transport companies, flour mills and bread manufacturers. Most of Australia's wheat is grown in a 'belt' stretching across the southern regions of Western Australia and South Australia, through inland Victoria and New South Wales to central Queensland. This area is known as Australia's wheat belt.

Dairy Industry

Australia produces more dairy products than are consumed by its population, and the extra produce is exported.

Alternative Energy Sources

Most Australians care about the environment and renewable energy sources are in demand. This has created growing interest in using power that comes from natural gas, solar cells, wind turbines and hydroelectric schemes.

Wind turbines

Fast fact

Australia exports around 70% of the total value of its agricultural, fishing and forestry production.

AMAZING NATURAL DIVERSITY

Australia was cut off from the rest of the world's landmass for over 100 million years. This allowed for a fascinating range of plants and animals to flourish, many of which are found nowhere else in the world.

Freycinet National Park in Tasmania

Islands

Did you know that Australia has over 8,000 islands? The State of Tasmania is an island south of the mainland of Australia, across Bass Strait. It is a place of stunning natural beauty. Other islands include South Australia's Kangaroo Island, which is an important sea lion sanctuary, and K'gari (formerly known as Fraser Island) in Queensland, which is the largest sand island in the world.

Feral Animals

Some feral animals such as cats, dogs, camels, rabbits, foxes, horses, pigs and cane toads were introduced to Australia. These introduced animals now negatively affect native animal populations and ecosystems.

Eucalypt Forests

Australia's most common tree is the eucalypt. There are hundreds of species of eucalypt, and most are native to Australia. The trees have oil-rich foliage that burns readily, contributing greatly to the spread of bushfires. However, some eucalypts have evolved ways to regenerate after the bushfire has passed.

Kookaburra

Eucalypt trees provide essential habitats and food for many animals. Some of the unique animals that inhabit Australia's forests and woodlands are the eastern grey kangaroo, the kookaburra, the Australian magpie, the echidna and several species of wallaby and possum. The most famous resident of the eucalypt tree is the koala.

The Koala

Koalas have lived in Australia's eucalypt forests and woodlands for millions of years. Sadly, land clearing, loss of habitat and climate change have impacted on koala numbers. In 2022, the koala was officially listed as an endangered animal.

The Daintree

Australia's Wet Tropics World Heritage Area in northeastern Queensland includes forested mountain ranges as well as lowland, tropical rainforests. The Daintree is one of the oldest rainforests left in the world, and it is home to some of the rarest and most spectacular flora and fauna. It is a complex web of diverse habitats, with creatures living at all levels of the forest, from the canopy to under the forest floor. One unusual creature found in the rainforests is the endangered southern cassowary.

Gondwana

The ancient supercontinent of Gondwana existed millions of years ago when Australia, Africa, New Guinea and other land masses were all joined together. The descendants of some of the plants from that time are still alive in Australia's rainforests.

The supercontinent of Gondwana broke apart to form the southern continents

Australia's Deserts

About 70% of mainland Australia, or a total of about 5.3 million square kilometres, is arid and semi-arid, while 18% is desert. Desert habitats include savannah grasslands, low woodlands, and sandy and rocky areas. These areas support animals such as bilbies, thorny devils, dingoes, emus, kangaroos, rock wallabies, snakes, spiders and smaller mammals.

Hundreds of bird species and reptiles live in Australia's deserts. The desert mammals have suffered a very high extinction rate, with animals such as the lesser bilby and desert rat-kangaroo gone forever.

There are 10 deserts in Australia:

1. Great Sandy Desert
2. Little Sandy Desert
3. Gibson Desert
4. Great Victoria Desert
5. Tanami Desert
6. Pedirka Desert
7. Simpson Desert
8. Tirari Desert
9. Strzelecki Desert
10. Sturt Stony Desert

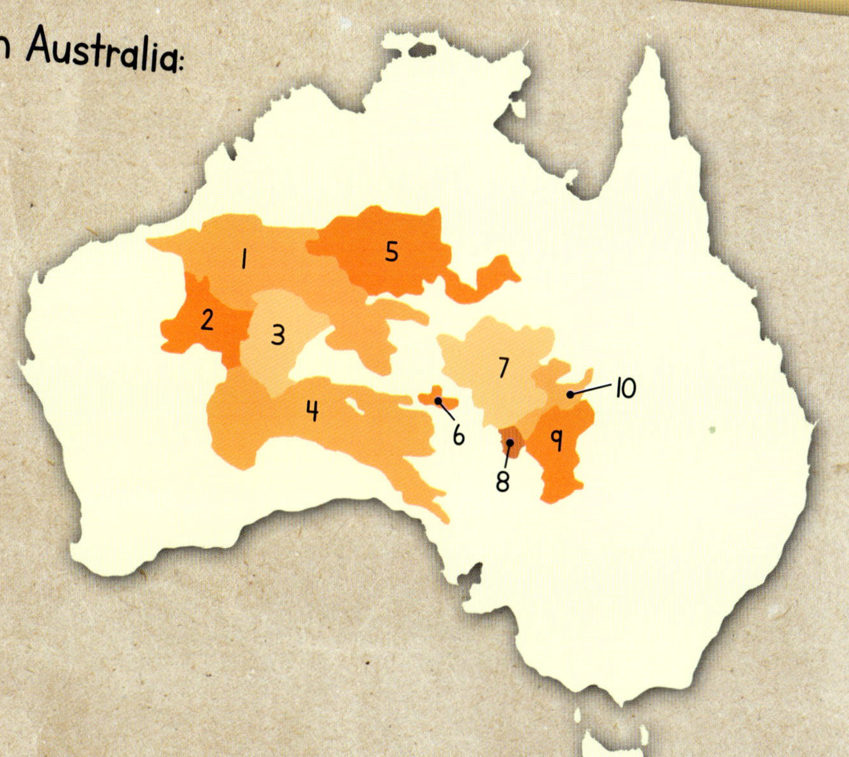

NATURAL WONDERS

Kakadu National Park

Kakadu National Park is about 240 kilometres east of Darwin and is the second-largest national park in Australia. Some of the ancient rocks in the park date back to over 2.5 billion years ago. Kakadu encompasses mangroves, coastal plains, sandstone cliffs, wetlands and forests. Each of these areas has its own array of wildlife, some of which is not found anywhere else. Kakadu has had a World Heritage listing since 1981.

Kakadu is on the traditional lands of the Bininj Mungguy Aboriginal people. In their Dreaming, the wonders of Kakadu were created by their ancestral and spirit figures.

Uluru

The Uluru-Kata Tjuta National Park

The Uluru-Kata Tjuta National Park has been a World Heritage Site since 1987 due to its natural and cultural value to Australia and the world. The magnificent rock formations represent the lives and works of creation ancestors and spirits.

Uluru is over 300 metres high and is thought to extend two kilometres underground. It measures more than nine kilometres around the base.

Kata Tjuta is a group of dome shaped rocks about 50 kilometres away from Uluru. The name means 'many heads' in Pitjantjatjara. The tallest dome of Kata Tjuta is 546 metres high, which is taller than Uluru.

The Anangu (comprising Pitjantjatjara and Yankunytjatjara people) are the traditional custodians of Uluru and Kata Tjuta.

Kata Tjuta

AUSTRALIA'S COAST AND OCEAN

Australia's Coast and Ocean

Australia's coastline measures about 34,000 kilometres. The coastal regions are where most Australians choose to live. Australia's coastal and ocean habitats encompass more than just the country's long sandy beaches and offshore islands and reefs. Along the coast are mangroves, lakes and river estuaries, rocky headlands and the fertile plains between the Great Dividing Range and the sea.

Wetlands

Australia recognises over 850 wetlands for their national importance. Australia's wetlands are vital for many migratory birds that travel from the Northern Hemisphere each year.

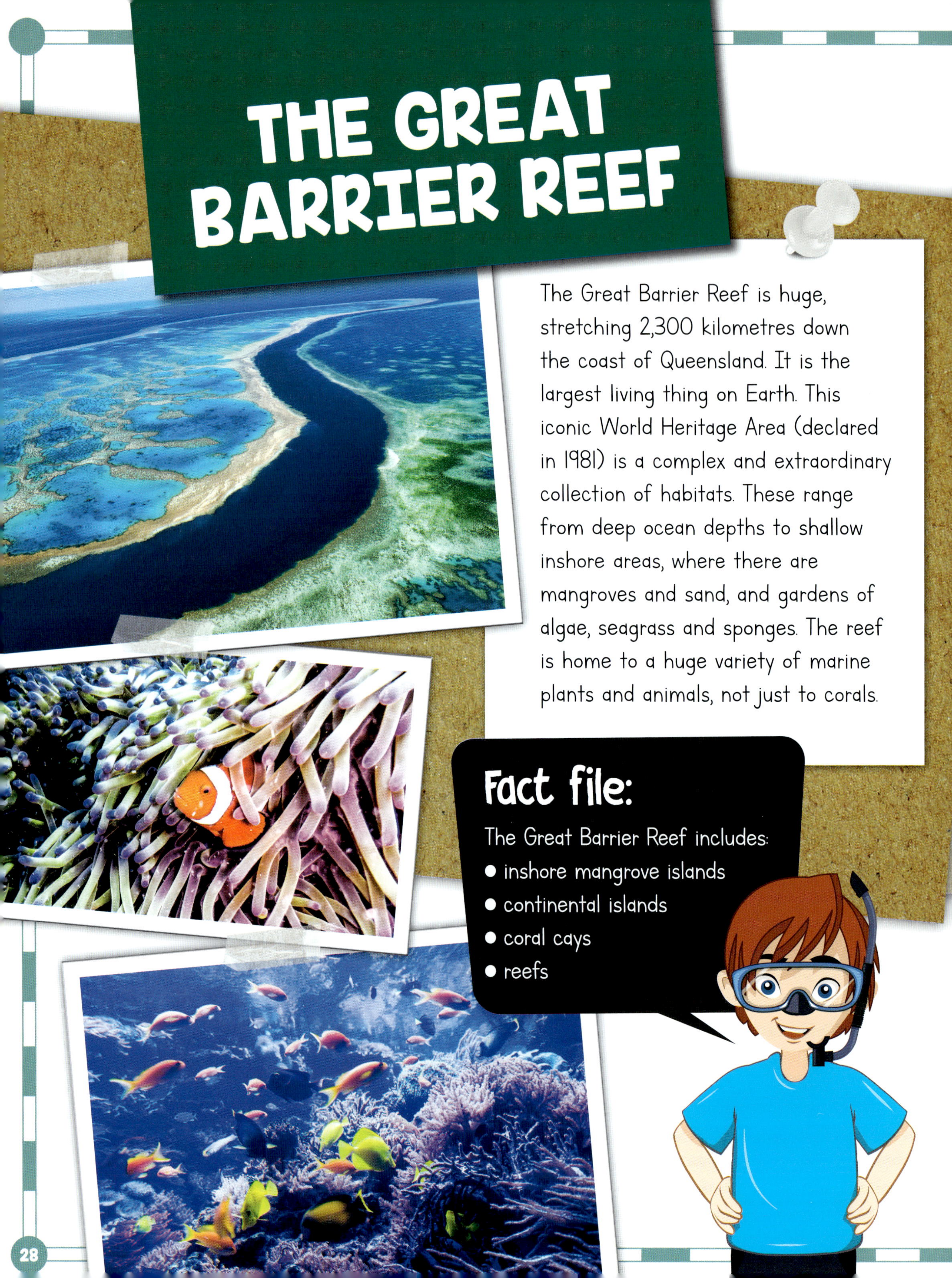

THE GREAT BARRIER REEF

The Great Barrier Reef is huge, stretching 2,300 kilometres down the coast of Queensland. It is the largest living thing on Earth. This iconic World Heritage Area (declared in 1981) is a complex and extraordinary collection of habitats. These range from deep ocean depths to shallow inshore areas, where there are mangroves and sand, and gardens of algae, seagrass and sponges. The reef is home to a huge variety of marine plants and animals, not just to corals.

Fact file:

The Great Barrier Reef includes:

- inshore mangrove islands
- continental islands
- coral cays
- reefs

SYDNEY HARBOUR

There are many iconic sights all around Australia, but Sydney Harbour is home to two of the most famous structures in the world: the Sydney Harbour Bridge and the Sydney Opera House.

Sydney Opera House

The Sydney Opera House is one of the most recognisable buildings in the world. In 1957, the NSW Government held a design contest to plan an opera house. The winner was Danish architect, Jørn Utzon. The shape of the building refers to shells and sails, inspired by the site's harbourside location near the Sydney Harbour Bridge. The construction began in March 1959, and Queen Elizabeth II opened the building in 1973. The Sydney Opera House has been a Word Heritage Site since 2007.

Sydney Harbour Bridge

The Sydney Harbour Bridge is recognised around the world as a symbol of Australia. Construction of the Sydney Harbour Bridge began on 28 July 1923. It was officially opened on 19 March 1932 by New South Wales Premier Jack Lang.

TRANSPORT

Australia has an extensive transport system, allowing people to get around by road, boat, rail and air. Most people arriving in the country do so by plane. Domestic flights are often the easiest way to cover Australia's vast distances, although there is also a good road system with highways linking regional towns and cities.

The Afghan Cameleers and The Ghan

The Afghan Cameleers, as they became known, came from Afghanistan and other parts of central and south-central Asia. They came to Australia in the 1800s to help deliver supplies across the Outback. They also carried building materials for the railway from Adelaide to Alice Springs, and for the telegraph line. Once the cameleers and their camel delivery services were no longer needed, the camels were released into the wild. The Ghan is a train that is named after the cameleers. It travels from Adelaide to Alice Springs.

Australia's rail system connects most populated areas and plays an important role in transporting large volumes of goods such as wheat, wool, coal and iron ore.

FLAGS AND SYMBOLS

Flags of Australia

The Australian National Flag was first flown on 3 September 1901.

The Australian Aboriginal Flag was first raised on 9 July 1971, National Aborigines' Day, at Victoria Square in Adelaide.

The Torres Strait Islander Flag was adopted in May 1992.

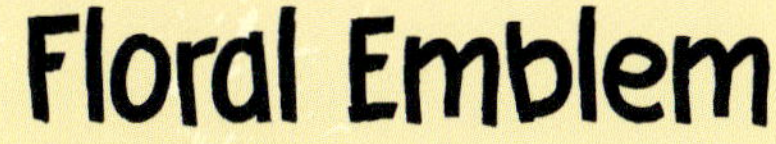

Floral Emblem

Australia's national floral emblem is the golden wattle, *Acacia pycnantha*.

National Anthem

Australia's National Anthem is *Advance Australia Fair*.

National Gemstone

Australia's national gemstone is the opal.

GLOSSARY

agriculture farming

architect someone who designs a building

arid region very dry area with low rainfall

dialect form of a language

ecosystem natural system that supports life within it

endangered may soon become extinct

endemic only found in a certain place

extinct no longer in existence

feral predators wild animals that kill and eat other animals

habitat place where plants and animals live

export send goods to overseas countries

film crew people who work on a film

film studio organisation that produces and distributes a film

gold rush rapid migration of people in search of gold

freight goods sent by rail, road, sea or air

on location filming done outside, rather than in a studio

species group of living things with similar characteristics

UNESCO World Heritage Site site judged by the United Nations to be of worth to the world

vulnerable may soon become endangered

wetlands areas of land that are temporarily or permanently covered by water

INDEX

ARCTIC OCEAN
GREENLAND
(DENMARK)
ALASKA (USA)
CANADA
ICELAND
FAROE ISLANDS
UNITED KINGDOM
IRELAND
FRANCE
NORTH PACIFIC OCEAN
UNITED STATES
NORTH ATLANTIC OCEAN
PORTUGAL
SPAIN
MOROCCO
ALGERIA
MEXICO
THE BAHAMAS
CUBA
MAURITANIA
MALI
CAPE VERDE
GUATEMALA
BELIZE
HONDURAS
EL SALVADOR
NICARAGUA
SENEGAL
THE GAMBIA
GUINEA-BISSAU
GUINEA
BURKINA FASO
COTE D'IVOIRE
GHANA
SIERRA LEONE
LIBERIA
COSTA RICA
PANAMA
VENEZUELA
GUYANA
SURINAME
FRENCH GUIANA
COLOMBIA
LINES ISLANDS
ECUADOR
PERU
BRAZIL
SOUTH PACIFIC OCEAN
COOK ISLANDS
FRENCH POLYNESIA
BOLIVIA
PARAGUAY
SOUTH ATLANTIC OCEAN
EASTER ISLAND
URUGUAY
ARGENTINA
CHILE
FALKLAND ISLANDS (UK)
SOUTH GEORGIA (UK)